AR 6.0
1 pt.

FEB 27 1996

DATE DUE

~~JUL 2 9 1996~~		
~~APR 2 0~~		

DEMC

Everything You Need to Know About

BEING A BIRACIAL/ BIETHNIC TEEN

Being from a biracial or biethnic family can raise many challenges in your life.

Everything You Need to Know About

BEING A BIRACIAL/ BIETHNIC TEEN

Renea D. Nash

THE ROSEN PUBLISHING GROUP, INC.
NEW YORK

Published in 1995 by The Rosen Publishing Group, Inc.
29 East 21st Street, New York, NY 10010

Copyright 1995 by The Rosen Publishing Group, Inc.

First Edition

Manufactured in the United States of America

Library of Congress Cataloging-in-Publication Data

Nash, Renea D.
    Everything you need to know about being a biracial/biethnic teen /
Renea D. Nash. — 1st ed.
        p.   cm. — (The need to know library)
    Includes bibliographical references and index.
    ISBN 0-8239-1871-8
    1. Children of interracial marriage—United States—Juvenile
literature.   2. Teenagers—United States—Life skills guides—
Juvenile literature.   3. Ethnicity in children—United States—
Juvenile literature.   I. Title.   II. Title: Being a
biracial/biethnic teen.   III. Series.
HQ77.9.N39   1995
306.84'6—dc20
                                                94-34644
                                                CIP
                                                AC

Contents

It is important to have pride in yourself and in your heritage.

Chapter 1

Discovering Your Identity

"I am not here to beg and plead with this racist society for a racial identity. I already have a place—an interracial place. I already have an identity—an interracial identity. I exist. I am real. I am here.

—*Bess Martinson*
Interracial Intercultural Pride

How often have you heard the question: "What are you?" Once? Twice? Hundreds? Chances are, you've heard it a lot. Growing up as a biracial child means that you're able to see the world as it truly is—multiracial. It also means that you have to answer questions about your race and your identity.

The world is quickly becoming a place where babies are being born to couples who are not of the same race. These couples are called interracial; their babies are biracial. Interracial and biracial are the most common terms used today. But that's changing too.

Before we address that, let's talk about a few important words.

Our bodies contain a great many substances called *genes*. We all have them. It doesn't matter what color you are on the outside, because genetically we're all the same species. We're all human. But something called *race* divides us into categories.

Race is a word used to group people based on shared physical characteristics. Unfortunately, racial differences cause many people to judge others unfairly. Some people wrongly believe that if they know someone's race, they know everything about that person.

Another way in which people can be classified is *ethnicity*. This term classifies people on the basis of physical characteristics and cultural traditions. It includes racial traits *and* national, religious, and language traits. The major ethnic groups in the United States are Irish, Italian, Polish, Jewish, Chinese, Japanese, and Hispanic.

Culture has to do with the customary beliefs, social forms, and material traits of an ethnic, racial, religious, national, or social group. For example, bowing is a custom practiced within Japanese culture. But Japanese children aren't born knowing that they should bow. Aspects of culture, like bowing, must be learned.

No matter what culture someone is from, he is the same as you: human.

It's All About People

It all seems confusing, but it really isn't. Read past these terms. Keep it simple in your mind by remembering that the words race, interracial, biracial, ethnic, multiracial, and culture all refer to the same thing—people.

Some people who ask, "What are you?" expect to hear a short answer. They want to hear that you're Italian, African-American, Hispanic, Japanese, Puerto Rican. They aren't prepared to accept "half" this or "part" that. But for you, a biracial teen, that's the truth!

In the last 20 years, the number of interracial marriages in the U.S. has increased from 310,000

Paula Abdul is one of many famous people who celebrate
different aspects of their mixed cultural heritage.

to more than 1.1 million. Since 1960, the number of
Jews marrying non-Jews has risen from 10 percent to
52 percent. Japanese-Americans marry people without
a Japanese heritage about 65 percent of the time.
Native Americans marry people who are not Native
American about 70 percent of the time. That's a large
number of interracial marriages.

And many of those couples are having children. There are also interracial couples who never marry but have children. No one knows the exact number of people in this group.

In your school, there may be other kids like you who come from mixed racial backgrounds. What about on television? Hollywood is full of entertainers of mixed racial and ethnic backgrounds, including actress-singer Jasmine Guy, who played on "A Different World." Mariah Carey, Anthony Quinn, the artist formerly known as Prince, and members of the pop musical group Cypress Hill all come from mixed racial and ethnic backgrounds—just like you do.

The size of the multiracial population in the United States is estimated at about five million by the Biracial Family Network in Chicago. The exact number is not known. This is because the government counts people every ten years in what's called a census. To make it easier to count the many millions of people in the United States, the government asks people to place themselves in a particular racial category. If your category is not listed on the form, you have to choose the box that is closest to your race or ethnic background. Your only other alternative is to check the box marked "Other." That means people like you, biracial people, can't be counted easily.

Not Enough Boxes

If your mother is Asian and your father is black,

do you mark the "Asian" box or the box marked "black"? What happens if you check both? That seems like the proper way to respond when you're biracial, doesn't it? In most cases, you are not allowed to check more than one box. As you saw at the beginning of this chapter, there are many different groups of people. Where are their boxes?

What about people whose parents are of different religions. Your mother may be Jewish and your father Catholic. What are you? Like interracial couples, interreligious couples and their children go through similar challenges.

Children of interracial couples are difficult for the government and society to classify. You have to "fit" or "belong" somewhere, according to society. Before 1989, the National Center for Health Statistics (NCHS) looked at the parents' race to determine the child's race. A child born to a white parent and a minority parent was said to be the race of the minority parent. If neither parent was white, the child was said to be of the father's race. This policy was changed in 1989. This may be in part because between 13 and 15 percent of all birth certificates do not have information about the father. So, the NCHS said the child was of the mother's race. (In Judaism, a child can be considered Jewish only if his mother is.)

How Parents Classify

Let's see now how parents classify their

Your identity is far more than just race or ethnicity, especially when you are of more than one race or ethnicity.

children. In 1980, more than half of children with one
black and one white parent were listed on government
surveys as "black." Also, 56 percent of Native
American/whites were listed as "American Indian."
Only 35 percent of Asian/whites were listed as
"Asian."

Some people try to write in mixed-race answers for
themselves or their children. Usually, however, only the
first race indicated is accepted. You're old enough to
realize that the world we live in believes in black and
white—not in the colors black and white, but in the
idea that things are either one way or the other. That
the answer is either yes or no, up or down, in or out.
But life isn't that simple, as any biracial teen who fills
in any application or form that asks about race knows.

Things are beginning to turn around. Many
multicultural organizations, like the San
Francisco–based Association of MultiEthnic
Americans (AMEA) and Atlanta's Project RACE
(Reclassify All Children Equally), are pushing for
the inclusion of a "mixed-race" category in the
official census by the year 2000. The AMEA
encourages persons of mixed race to claim their
whole identity, to stand up and be counted for who
they are. It also makes society aware of the issues.

Project RACE was formed in 1991 with the
objective of requiring a multiracial category on all
forms asking for racial data. As a result of their
efforts, school districts in Atlanta, Cincinnati,

Ohio, and DeKalb County, Georgia, added such a category for all students.

But discovering your identity is about more than having your own box to check.

Many different words are used to describe people whose makeup is multiracial. The list is very long. Interracial, biracial, multiracial, biethnic, mixed, mulatto, and even rainbow are all textbook terms. There are other, negative terms that you have probably heard, but they are most likely used by people who are ignorant of the value of being biracial.

But discovering your identity is more than having a term that describes you.

It's about becoming comfortable with all aspects of your heritage—racial, ethnic, and religious. It is not necessary for you to deny part of your background to please others. It is possible for both parts of your background to complement each other to give you a broad view of society and your place in it. You have a unique contribution to make in an increasingly multicultural world.

The Best of Two Worlds

In fact, as a biracial child, you have the best of two worlds. If you have parents who are from different cultures and they have taught you aspects of both and practice aspects of both, you are a fully enriched person! You are truly a bicultural person. You are better equipped to get along both at home and abroad.

Everyone wants to belong, but sometimes it seems that ethnicity divides us.

Biracial children often have better skills to get along with other races. Chances are likely that you get along with kids from all kinds of racial and ethnic backgrounds because you are comfortable with more than one ethnicity. Unfortunately, others might not get along with you. Some biracial teens say they experience problems with other kids. Racism still exists in our society.

A counselor at a Southwest junior high school had a biracial student, Tiffany, who came to her office in tears. She was being teased by a few black girls about having a "white" mother. "They don't even know my mother," Tiffany cried to the counselor. "She's cool."

Tiffany really wanted to be friends with these girls. Being part black and part white, she felt it was important to be accepted by them. What did Tiffany do to resolve the problem? She invited one of the girls to her house. The girl got to see just how "cool" Tiffany's white mother was. She passed the word to the others, and Tiffany was welcomed into their circle of friends.

Obviously, being accepted was important enough to Tiffany for her to try to make friends with the girls. Prejudice and racism can be strong feelings. Not everyone can be turned around. We all have to look at each situation and decide what's "worth it" and what's not worth it. For Tiffany, it was "worth it."

Everybody wants to be liked, especially teenagers. Having friends makes you feel good about yourself. We all want to be liked, loved, and made to feel part of the crowd. How far should we go to be liked? Will you pretend not be biracial? Will you try to hide your parents? Will you try to act a certain way to fit in?

Growing up isn't easy. The best advice that you will hear from biracial teens in this book is, "Be yourself."

Parents Have Problems Too

Being a parent isn't easy. Being a parent of a biracial child carries certain challenges. The way in which the world looks at race and identity forces your parents to be concerned about you. Not for your safety, but for your self-identity. Your mother and father want you to be happy and confident about your identity. They want you to be proud of being you.

Every interracial family handles its racial identity differently. Some parents say, "My child is a human above everything else. The color of his or her skin doesn't matter." Some parents choose to raise their children with the identity of the parent of color. And some parents say, "My child is biracial so my child will have two racial identities."

Communication

Professionals say the adults in your life play a major part in helping you answer the questions, "Who am I?" and "Where do I fit in?" Biracial teens and adults say that parents (or a trusted adult) can prepare teens simply by communicating with them. Do you and your parent or parents talk? Do you talk about your racial identity?

Talking to a parent is tough for some teens. How do you talk about something as personal as your racial identity? You may want to start by asking how your parents met. Then ask about their decision to have you. Then ask if they ever talked about how you would look or what race you'd identify with. It may seem like a silly question, but it'll spark a conversation. Pretty soon, you'll be talking about many of the issues that you're curious about.

Share experiences with them and feelings you've had or are having. If you feel, as some teens do, that "it's no big deal to be biracial," tell them that too. If a parent is not around, talk to a big brother or sister, an aunt, a grandmother, a friend's parent, a teacher, a counselor, or a religious leader. Or talk to another biracial teen. Talking helps, and it's fun to share.

Chapter 2

This Is Who I Am

When you were a small child, you probably played with other kids in your neighborhood. Do you remember what color they were? You probably didn't think of them as being of any particular color or race. They were just the kids.

As you got older, you probably started to see a difference, to compare people. By the age of seven or eight, most children know their ethnic labels: "I'm African-American," "I'm Japanese-American," "I'm Mexican."

By your teenage years, you start thinking, "What does it mean to be black? Hispanic? Cambodian? Puerto Rican?" You begin to understand things better. You start to hang out with others who are from outside of your community. For example, when you hang out with people of other races it makes you realize some of

Being biracial or biethnic means having the chance to learn about two or more different heritages.

the differences that exist between various cultures. For instance, choices (and preparation) of food, styles of clothing, music, literature, and language used in a community are often shaped by the culture of that community.

One more thing happens. You start worrying: about your appearance, dating, and your future. You know those thoughts: What do I want to be when I grow up? Where did this zit come from? Whom will I marry? All these things are related to the development of your identity.

Racial Identity

Racial identity is defined as "pride in one's racial and cultural background." It's important for several reasons. It helps to shape your attitudes about yourself and others, and it helps to form the way you deal with others and the way they react to you.

The development of racial identity is more complicated and can be more difficult for biracial teens. You belong to or have several different racial identities. Some people believe that being biracial can cause problems in developing a true self-identity because you won't be able to "fit in" with any one group.

Growing up biracial, you go through several stages on your way to achieving racial identity. Those steps involve realizing that you belong in some racial category. They involve trying to decide which category that is. And they involve being happy with your decision.

All biracial children—because of their unique racial makeup—go through these steps.

Nancie went through each of them. She's proud of her mixed heritage. You'll see how she developed through each step and what she says about each.

Belonging

"I belong to this group," was the first step.

People reach this stage at a young age. They become aware that they belong to a particular ethnic group, but they're really not much concerned. Children tend to have a sense of who they are based on self-esteem and feelings of self-worth that they have developed and learned from their family. It has very little to do with ethnic background. Basically, they're just happy kids who enjoy playing with other happy kids.

"I am the product of an interracial marriage. My father is Mexican. He was born and raised in Mexico, where he played professional baseball. My mom was born in Ellensburg, Washington. She is white. She was on a trip to Pueblo during her vacation in Mexico when she met my father at the hotel that they were both staying at. They married shortly after they met, even though neither one of them could speak the other's

Toys have begun to reflect the fact that society is made up of many different kinds of people.

language. The community where we lived was fairly mixed with Hispanics and Anglos. When I started school, I realized I was different from the majority of the kids. I didn't look like either my mother or my father. My mom is blonde with hazel eyes and a fair complexion. My father is the exact opposite: dark hair and a dark complexion. I'm somewhere in between.

"From very early in school, kids teased me and called me a half-breed. Well, I never took it to heart or even realized it was anything bad until I was older. My parents had always taught me that I was lucky to have such a diverse background. I was happy to tell people I was born in Mexico."

Choosing

The second step: "How do I choose?"

This is where you start to feel a little concerned about your particular ethnic group. At this stage, you are pushed to choose an identity. You may be pressed by friends, peers, family, or social groups so they can better fit you in. Does the question, "What do you consider yourself?" sound familiar?

Biracial people have two ways to go. One is to choose a multiethnic existence. This means that both of your parents will have a heavy influence on your life. It could mean learning different languages and practicing a variety of traditions.

The other way is to choose one parent's heritage over the other.

This stage can be a time of crisis. Several factors can help in making such a choice: status, social support, and personal factors.

Status involves the kind of neighborhood you live in and how your family's income compares to those around you.

Social support factors involve whether your relatives (grandparents and so on) and friends accept your interracial family.

Finally, personal factors. What are your physical features? Are you willing to learn and practice a parent's native language, traditions, or customs? Can you do so freely in your home, or is it forbidden? Are you mature enough to make a choice and stay with it?

All three of these factors play major roles in helping biracial persons make racial identity choices.

Someone who is African-American and German may identify himself as black. Why? Maybe his skin color is closer to black than white. Maybe he grew up in a predominantly black neighborhood. Maybe his German mother's parents did not accept a "black" grandchild. Someone else who is African-American and German may consider himself German. Why? Maybe his skin color is closer to white than black. Maybe he grew up in Germany. Maybe his parents speak fluent German. See the difference in how these factors can help you choose?

Choosing a multiethnic identity can be difficult. It requires knowledge and understanding of each culture. It also involves your parents' support, a lot of studying, and living a multicultural life. Only *you* can decide if you truly can be bicultural.

For Nancie, the years between the third and eighth grades were the hardest.

"It was more difficult for me to identify with a specific group. At my school, the Hispanic kids hung around together and the Anglo kids hung around together. I leaned toward the Anglo group because they were more from the same economic background. Also, they were the ones who lived in my neighborhood.

"This made the Hispanic kids resentful, not to

mention the fact that I was also a teacher's kid. The Hispanic girls were especially hostile. They couldn't understand me. I was supposed to be like them, but I wasn't. That was hard for me. I wanted to belong with everyone, but I didn't. My mother's parents along with my own parents gave me privileges and opportunies that other kids in my area—Anglo or Hispanic—didn't have. I traveled to Europe, and I went to plays with my grandfather, who was a drama professor at California State-Fresno. I rarely spent my summer at home like the other kids. That was hard for me. I always knew I would go to college when the majority of kids in my area were wondering if they were going to graduate from high school."

Do you see how Nancie's story follows these steps? Do you see how she made decisions on her identity based on her family's status and the surroundings?

Whom Must You Please?

The next step: "Do I have to please everyone?"

The answer is no. This stage includes confusion and guilt over having to decide between both heritages. Some people experience self-hatred and lack of acceptance from one or more groups. For example, a biracial teen may be ashamed, embarrassed, or afraid to have friends meet his or her parent whose racial background is different from others in the neighborhood or school.

He or she may feel guilty and angry at this situation. What happens? The teen either stays at this level or has to learn to appreciate both parental cultures. At this stage, support from your parents, a trusted adult, a support group, or other biracial teens is crucial in helping to resolve the problem. Experiencing this much guilt is not healthy.

Nancie didn't spend long at this stage. Why? She had strong support from her family. There is no set amount of time that you will spend at each of these stages. It really depends on you and your environment. Nancie eased through feelings of confusion and guilt. She did experience some pain.

"Not fitting in is normal for teenagers, I know that. In high school, the groups were still separated. I didn't associate much with the Hispanic groups. My friends were all Anglo—all born in the United States and all having both parents who were born here as well as probably their parents before them. I wouldn't say that all their families were prejudiced, but the majority had some feeling against anyone who wasn't like them. But I didn't count, because part of me was like them and that was better than nothing.

"During these years, I was exposed to all sorts of prejudices, mainly because I didn't appear to be a minority. Everything from racial slurs and comments to complete racial hatred were a part of my experience. For a while, I was silent, but that

A good place to turn for help in dealing with the difficulties of being biracial or biethnic is a peer support group.

didn't last long. I became very vocal about the offensiveness of people's comments and racial jokes. But I was always told: 'We don't mean you.' That was the hardest part of being biracial, and it still is."

Like Nancie, you'll get to these last two stages: "This is who I am" and "I do fit in."

The Stage of Appreciation

"This is who I am." You'll come to appreciate your rich identity. Biracial teens at this stage begin to learn about their racial/ethnic heritages and cultures. But they still tend to identify with one group.

Remember the black/German person we talked about earlier. He can consider himself black *and* seek knowledge of his German ancestry and participate in traditions and customs. That's appreciation. That's pride in all of you!

For example, Nino is half Italian and half black-Puerto Rican. If he were asked, "In a war between blacks and whites, which side would you be on?" his answer might be, "I'd try to make peace between the two."

Integration

The final stage is integration—"I do fit in." At this stage, biracial people experience wholeness and integration. They tend to recognize and value all of their ethnic identities. They are secure as to who they are.

From Nancie's story, you'll also see that integration doesn't end after junior high or high school. You don't just wake up one morning and say, "I've done it! I feel part of the group!" As you grow older, you change. Society also changes. Attitudes, however, sometimes remain the same, and you find yourself fighting battles you thought you had already won. But that happens with everybody. It's what makes life so interesting.

"Even in college where people were supposed to be open and intellectual, the same attitudes continued. The Hispanic groups on campus still treated me the way every other Hispanic group had treated me: like I didn't belong because I was only half Mexican and couldn't possible know or feel the way they felt about racial prejudice. That is a big problem with being biracial.

"It's not a problem of knowing who you are and where you came from. But it's others who can't fit you in a category. My parents raised me to be proud of who I am, and I am. The benefits of having two cultures far outweigh anything I experienced in growing up. We live in a society of many races and cultures. I feel that I have a better understanding of the world. Someday I plan to raise my own children with their heritage. They will know our culture and where they came from as well."

Nancie believes that biracial teens should be proud of their background. Like her, you should focus on building a positive self-esteem. "You should concentrate on making everything equal; race comes second."

Let's briefly review: (1) Biracial people tend to have questions about their identity. (2) A number of factors influence a biracial teen's identity choice. (3) Choosing can result in feelings of guilt and disloyalty to a parent. (4) Integration is healthy. (5) The most difficult time of adjustment and identity confusion is when you're trying to make choices.

Number 5 is probably where you are now. Right? You're not alone. That's why it's so important to read books like this and seek support from an adult, brothers or sisters, or support groups.

As you saw in Nancie's story, many biracial teens have handled the process of biracial identity development with success. Like Nancie, they've grown up to be well-adjusted, happy adults.

Nancie commented along the way that your parents help you develop a healthy self-concept. They can provide the basics such as love, support, and self-esteem development *and* the knowledge of both—or all—of your racial/ethnic identities.

Other biracial adults agree with Nancie. Their parents showed them the positive aspects of their unique identities and of being biracial. They too encourage you to take pride in who you are and to share your pride with others. You have the best of both worlds.

Chapter 3

The Role of the Parent

Families come in many sizes. You have the "Brady Bunch," complete with mother, father, six kids, a dog, and a maid. On the other hand, you have "Thea's" or "Blossom's" family with a single parent raising three children.

Families come in many forms. Two people who have a child together but never marry, two people who adopt a child, foster parents, and a divorced parent with children are all families.

Families also come in many colors. Your family is living proof. For any family, no matter what size, form, or color, the addition of a baby is challenging. And some members of society often challenge the family portrait created by interracial families, which adds more pressures. Most stories told by interracial families are positive. Some are not.

Some face discrimination when trying to rent or purchase a place to live. Some report the loss of

It might be helpful to write down your thoughts and feelings about being biracial or biethnic.

friends. Others receive cold treatment from coworkers and family members. Some interracial couples even report receiving poor service in places like restaurants or theaters. Most can give accounts of stares, whispers, and questions. So you can see that your parent or parents had to do some coping of their own.

Society's View

Debra and Bill, an interracial couple, have three children. Their first child gave them their first experience with how society was going to view their children.

"The little child looked white," Debra laughs,

"and here I am, black as black can be." Since it was their first child, the young couple didn't know what color to expect. They also didn't expect what happened following the birth of Jillesa: The nurses didn't believe she belonged to Debra! The baby looked like a white child. Other mothers and fathers of biracial children have reported similar experiences.

"She looked really, really white," Debra says of her daughter, who is now of a beautiful beige complexion. "That was really hard on me. I would say, 'Give me my child, please!'"

Debra's humor and honesty are signs that she is and always has been comfortable with her interracial family. "I just thought we were going to have kids," she says. "We didn't think about whether they were going to look black or white— as long as they didn't come out half-and-half like little zebras."

Debra and Bill tell their children that they are black. Why? "Because when you're asked on forms, there's no category for mixed kids," Debra explains. "There's black, white, Hispanic, Native American, or Other, but no 'None of your business.'" Some parents of interracial children feel left out in checking the box marked "Other."

Debra and Bill seem happy and well adjusted to life as an interracial family. However, some may see them as being too comfortable or too passive about the way society views their children.

There are many opinions about biracial children. No one can agree on what to call you or how you should be classified or raised. In 1984, the first conference on biracial children was held in New York City, sponsored by the Council on Interracial Books for Children. It was attended by parents of interracial families, scholars, and others who research interracial families. They talked about developing positive self-identity in interracial children. They also talked about the need for more resources such as school books that reflect the interracial reality. The big question was: How do parents of interracial children raise normal, healthy children in a society that views interracial unions as abnormal and harmful?

The answer is not easy. Nothing is simple when you're dealing with humans. Interracial families want to be treated like "normal" families. They all agreed that their families were not the problem: It was society's viewing their families as abnormal that was the problem.

Books Can Help

Your parents may be struggling with some of the same issues you're facing, as well as concerns of their own. Their concerns may include the absence of positive role models in books, on television, or in the movies. When was the last time you opened a storybook or a textbook and found a family like yours? Wouldn't such books be helpful in understanding racial and cultural differences? Stories about the hurt of racism or about mixed families can help biracial children work through their feelings. Reading stories about teens like you or parents like yours, no matter what your racial or cultural heritage, helps you gain a sense of pride. It helps you feel that your uniqueness is real. It helps to promote self-esteem.

A few books that include interracial families are available in the library. The number is small. You may choose to cope by writing a children's book of your own. That might be an especially good idea if you have younger brothers or sisters who will have to walk the same road you're traveling now.

All people are faced with the existence of racism. People who are biracial, like you, are likely to have to deal with it on a very personal level. You are likely to face the same racist attitudes that any minority teen does. In addition, biracial teens must cope with out-siders who view your normal, loving, strong family as strange.

These people may be teachers, coaches, counselors, neighbors, relatives. Whoever they are, they often blame any problems you may have while growing up on your interracial family. This is pure ignorance.

Biased Standards

You also have to deal with a society that holds

white people as the standard of beauty. Think about it: the Barbie Doll, fashion model Cindy Crawford, actor Luke Perry. This standard affects all children of color as well as all biracial children.

What about the biracial little girl who has a strong attachment to her white mother but does not have the same blond hair. How often have you been asked if you're adopted, or why you don't look like your father or mother? How did you feel? Children wanting to identify with both parents can be hurt by society's rejection of their racial duality. It's important to have your own beauty affirmed.

Listen to a conversation between a black mother and her biracial child as it was told by the mother in an article appearing in a 1992 *Glamour* magazine.

"Your skin is brown, right, mommy?" the daughter said.

"That's right, my skin is brown," the mother replied.

"I wish you were white like me," the little girl said.

Trying not to sound unnerved, the mother responded, "Your skin isn't white."

"Yes, it is," the child replied. "It's the same color as daddy's. I don't want to talk about it anymore."

Changing Views

The racial issues that the mother and father had

You'd be surprised at how many people have more than one ethnic heritage.

regularly confronted had left their daughter confused. The mother had taught her daughter that black was as good and as beautiful as white. When her daughter pointed to pictures of white models and commented on their beauty, the mother had pointed to brown-skinned models and praised both. Despite the mother's efforts to answer her biracial daughter's questions, the terms black and white meant more than just colors to the child. That day, the woman's daughter chose to be white.

In other situations, the daughter had associated being black with being powerless. She had seen homeless black people and blacks in poverty, and she didn't want to identify with with that part of society.

The author wrote: "Because of scenes like these, I understand why my daughter told me that she was white, and why she wished that I were, too. She was wishing that I had a way to pass into the easy life as well; she could already see that life as a black woman is harder."

The article ends with another conversation that took place a few weeks later.

"You're brown, right, Mom?" the child asked.

"That's right," the mother replied.

Her daughter held out her own arm. "But I'm brown . . . and white."

"Yes," the mother replied, hugging her daughter. "I guess that sounds right."

The mother was satisfied with this compromise and said she hoped that time and love would make her daughter strong enough to bear any hurt that came her way.

It is the hope of many parents of interracial families to be able to raise their children successfully in a society filled with racism, intolerance, and hatred. But how does a single white parent help her Iranian-white son deal with racism? She hasn't gone through life as a minority. These parents face the same task that faces all minority parents: to make their children feel secure and loved and prepare them for the harsh reality of racism.

A child who is not given a clear grounding in his or her cultural backgrounds may be resentful. Parents need to have a clear understanding about racism and how it impacts their children's lives. An African-American man talks about his interracial daughters. "I just feel that my girls would have all the tools they needed to succeed in life if they would 'see' themselves as I saw myself growing up as a child—a minority.

"In this world, I believe that I would be doing a disservice to my children not to give them an 'identity' as *everyone* in *every* form wants to know: What are you? If my girls tried to be accepted as Anglo, I felt that this would only be setting them up for criticism, frustration, and maybe more."

Communication

The conclusion is simple: Communication is the key in interracial families. Talk to your parents or to another adult about your identity. Understand that a parent who is not biracial or a minority has not had the same experiences in life as you have, but that they do know there are issues to be dealt with. You should be able to raise questions, express anger, and work through your feelings with someone. You must deal with racism and be ready to cope with negative reactions toward your interracial family.

You might want to suggest to your parents that

they talk to your teachers about some of the things you are experiencing. Teachers often go to seminars and training programs or are asked to read literature that might help them provide supportive environments. Together, your parents and teachers may be able to create a program including people of various cultural and racial heritages. With the new emphasis on celebrating cultural diversity, many schools have made such classes mandatory.

Teachers can be insensitive to biracial children. For example, one teacher asked an Asian-American/white teenager to write some Chinese characters on the board. The teen had been born and raised in New York and had never learned her father's native language. The teacher's unfortunate assumption made the student very uncomfortable. Making assumptions of that kind is called stereotyping. Stereotyping may be particularly disturbing for multiethnic teens who are entirely "American" in culture.

If you don't feel comfortable confronting your teacher or administrator, ask a parent, a family member, or the school counselor to go with you. Shouldn't teachers be confronted just like teenagers?

Living in a mixed community also makes life easier for interracial families. Biracial children are able to have friends of all races and become comfortable with a variety of children.

Support Groups

You may want to set up a support group made up of other biracial teens at school or in your neighborhood. Many support groups are available. Your family may want to join one. Or you can set up your own. First, find members, or other people like you. Post notices on community bulletin boards and at school, church, or synagogue. Place ads in local newspapers. Talk to other teens about starting a support group. You also can contact interracial membership organizations for ideas.

Then find a place to meet. Churches, synagogues, or community centers often offer their meeting rooms free of charge. Once a group is established and meetings are arranged, you may want to subscribe to the newsletters of other interracial organizations. Learn from them. Start your own newsletter.

Remember, ultimately you—the interracial teen—decide your identity.

Proud Achievers

So far we've talked about challenges or problems. The truth of the matter is that most interracial children become healthy adults. One study that focused on interracial children from black/white unions found interesting results. It reported that interracial children tend to be achievers with a strong sense of self. They are

Interracial teens often feel comfortable around many different kinds of people.

comfortable in predominantly white or black situations. They are proud of their mixed background and tolerant of people's differences. The same can probably be said about any racial or ethnic combination.

Are those things you've noticed about yourself? Do you feel comfortable in settings that include people of varied racial or cultural backgrounds? Are you always the one in your circle of friends who promotes peace when races clash? Chances are these are traits in you. If they haven't surfaced yet, they probably will. If you and an adult communicate openly and honestly about your racial identity, it is likely to happen.

The world is strange. On one hand, society

brags about being so diverse. On the other hand, society often rejects interracial unions. You, as an interracial teen, must work through these obvious conflicts. Ultimately, however, such problems will be solved only when racism no longer exists in our society. When will that be?

Society is quickly changing into one where the minority population will be the majority. Racial identity may not be much of an issue in the year 2000. In fact, parents are banking on just that.

Remember Debra and Bill? Debra says, "When they grow up, it won't be a problem. At least, I hope it won't be a problem for them. I think it'll work itself out." She then looks into the eyes of her oldest, five-year-old Jillesa. "I think it's kind of neat. I mean, they look at their daddy, then they look at their mommy—and we're two extremes. One is white as white can be, and the other is black as black can be. I think that's special."

No parent—single, married, divorced, or widowed—and no adult—adopted parent, foster parent, or guardian—will argue with that.

Chapter 4

Having Pride

Racial identity is about having pride—being proud. When you have pride, it's easier to fight racism directed toward you. When you have pride, it's easier to answer questions about your identity. When you have pride, it's easier to know where you fit in.

Biracial children who grow up to be happy adults give their parents a lot of credit. They believe that they had the best of their mother's culture and the best of their father's culture all rolled into one. To them, the beauty of being biracial is that you have the ability and the right to embrace more than one culture. That's really who you are, isn't it?

Simply having an awareness of your parents' heritage is not necessarily enough. You can experience all the cultures that make up your unique racial background. You can gain that experience in many different ways.

Martin Luther King, Jr. believed in pride in one's heritage. He fought for equality of all people.

You can learn about your ancestors from reading history books in your school or local library. You can look at old family photo albums. You can talk to your grandparents and your greatgrandparents. They know a lot!

Experience Your Background

For some biracial people, experiencing their cultural backgrounds may mean learning to speak another language. It may mean learning and practicing a variety of customs and traditions. It may mean attending and participating in special events such as parades, dances, and fiestas that

help celebrate the uniqueness of the culture. It may
mean being exposed to different music and rituals and
customs. Teens from interreligious backgrounds might
try to go through similar experiences to understand
their backgrounds fully.

Parents or other family members can provide these
kinds of experiences for you, or you can do so on your
own. Experts, as well as other biracial people, agree
that it is more healthy for you and your family if these
experiences are ongoing and happen as a family, beginning early in childhood. They also agree that kids with
a true "biracial" identity grow up to be even happier
than biracial kids who grow up with a "single-race"
identity. Basically, psychologists agree that it is un-
healthy to deny completely a part of your heritage.

If you haven't been having a true "biracial" experience, you're probably thinking, "I'm a teenager. It's too
late now." Well, it's not too late. It's never too late. You
and your family members can begin exploring your
racial/ethnic backgrounds at any point in time, the
sooner the better.

You may wonder what changes will occur in your life
if you begin to become "truly" biracial. What will
happen if you start accepting each part of your racial
heritage? What will happen if you allow each to
become an active part of you and your life? You'll
achieve a sense of pride, a sense of identity. Then,
answering a question like "What are you?" will be as
natural as answering "How old are you?"

Having pride doesn't mean that you won't get tired

of hearing that question. Nancie said that she experienced the same childhood attitudes when she entered college! So it may be something you'll have to learn to live with. It may be frustrating. But showing that frustration again and again takes more energy than simply answering the question. And when you do answer it, answer it with confidence.

Whatever your answer, more questions are likely to follow. Handle them with the same confidence as the first. If more come, be more confident.

Talk to Your Parents

There is a chance that one of your parents may feel that you've rejected his or her side of your heritage. There is a chance that members of the race you're identifying with won't accept you as a legitimate member. What do you do?

These possibilities are the reason it is important to discuss your unique racial identity with your family. Remember the conversation in Chapter 1? Take it further. Discuss prejudice and racism in our society and ways in which you can respond to discrimination. Talk about how you should identify yourself on forms at school, if you should check one box or two—or none! Discuss your own concerns, fears, or anxieties if you have any. Discuss skin color, hair texture, and your other

Young children are rarely prejudiced toward their playmates.

physical features. Discuss your feelings with your brothers and sisters, and let them express theirs to you.

Share with your friends what it's like being biracial and in an interracial family. You may even want to make it a subject of a report or speech. Share it with your teachers and other adults you come in contact with, especially if you sense tension. If *you* don't educate people about racial harmony, who will? If you and those like you don't, people will remain ignorant. Ignorance leads to fear. Fear leads to racism and discrimination.

If you can't talk out your feelings or have no one to listen to your feelings, write them out. You can write them out and give them to a parent. Or you can write them out for yourself—and give them to no one!

If you're having trouble learning the pride that's inside you, look to groups like I-Pride, or a trusted adult, or a parent. Never underestimate the power of looking for support right in your own home. You will find that a parent can be the best source of help and support.

If you're just full of pride and a lot of success discovering your identity, you may want to help other biracial teens do so. You'll be surprised that you'll feel even better!

Chapter 5

The Best of Both Worlds

The most challenging part of being biracial is also perhaps the best part of being biracial: having more than one race or culture to identify with. That's how other teenagers look at it. That's how their parents look at it. That's how you should look at it.

There are many different types of people in this world. That's why we say the world is diverse. In this culturally diverse society, you're the only one who can really celebrate true racial harmony. You're living proof; you have the best of both worlds.

The Wade Family

This chapter is about one family who believe just that. Meet the Wades. They include three girls, Mycah, Sarah, and Leah, and their parents,

Jill and Micah. Jill is white, Micah is black. In 1993, they celebrated their 20th wedding anniversary.

People told them they shouldn't have children because it would be hard on the kids. Jill and Micah were in love. They married, and three children later they are the kind of family storybooks and G-rated movies are made of. One of Leah's friends calls them the "Brady Bunch," after a TV series about an almost-perfect family.

Jill is a cool mom. On the weekends, she gives her beeper to her daughters so that their friends can reach them (and so can she). Micah is a devoted father who teases his daughters about their baggy attire and hard-to-understand slang. The three teenage daughters are self-confident and attractive, and each has her own dynamic personality.

They are like average teenage girls. They fight. They talk on the phone. They like boys. In some ways, they are unlike average teenagers. They have high self-esteem. They communicate openly with their parents and each other. They are sure of their identity.

Mycah is the oldest. She has sort of set the pace for her two younger sisters. "It's not that big a deal for me," she says of being biracial. "I know it is for some people, but I'm not in anguish about it. Oh, no, I'm biracial! I mean, what's the big deal?" That's her attitude. She's always had it. She has confidence in herself. Her belief in herself and her racial background is stronger than prejudice. She relies on her mental strength, and for her it works.

Sarah is the middle sister. She has faced rejection from a group she feels she belongs to. "I want to be friends with everyone," she says. "I really go out of my way so they can get to know me." It works for her.

Mycah disagrees with that attitude. "I feel, if they don't want to be friends with you because you're biracial, then they're not worth it. I don't want to be friends with them! You have to be yourself."

Leah is the youngest. She once told her mother that she was glad to be biracial because she fits in with both white and black people. She moves from one racial group to the other with very little concern. "When I'm with white friends, I feel like I'm white and I fit in," she says. "When I'm with black girls, I feel like I fit in too."

Mycah

"I never think of myself as being different when I am with a group of people unless someone says something. Then I'm taken aback, and I realize, 'Oh, so you see me that way!' This doesn't happen very often. I just try to get along with everyone. I basically have friends who are white, black, Mexican, and Asian. I have had boyfriends in the past who were both black and white. I don't really think about what they are when I meet them. I am either interested in them or not! I think that by having both my parents raise me together, I feel comfortable with all races. I'm very happy to be biracial, and so far I've had very few problems because of it. Mostly, I have had good experiences."

Sarah

"I am mostly attracted to black guys, although I have had white boyfriends before. I look more African-American than my sisters. That's probably why I attract African-American boys more often. My dad has a good relationship with us girls, and I think that he gives us a good image of African-American guys. Therefore, I am comfortable with them. Since all three of us attend the same high school, we have many of the same friends. Ironically, we have several friends who are also biracial. In fact, we went to a retreat last year that was designed to make everyone aware of the many races. It was a very emotional weekend, and I believe everyone came home with a new appreciation for the other races."

Leah

"I love being biracial. I understand and get along with both races. When I am with my father's

Biracial/biethnic teens often have high self-esteem.

family, I laugh and understand their humor and
problems. And when I'm with my mother's family,
I laugh and understand them too! I think that I get
the best of both worlds. I've had a few boyfriends
back in the third and fourth grades; usually they
were white. But now I'm in the ninth grade and I
have my first kind of real boyfriend; he's black. I
like him a lot, partly because he is taller than me
and we both play basketball. Basketball is my first
love. I just go and play the game without really
thinking about racial things. When I do think
about it, I realize that I am out there playing with
girls of every race, and we are having a great time!
Most of my girlfriends are white. In fact, my best

friend is white. But I also have girlfriends who are black and Mexican."

As you see, the girls have friends and boyfriends from a variety of backgrounds. Dating sometimes can cause mixed feelings—especially from your boyfriend/girlfriend's parents. It's always a good idea to talk about how your interracial dating will affect the other's family. It may not be a concern at all. If it is, then the two of you will have to make some choices.

Mycah, Sarah, and Leah also have many biracial friends. Some of them are having problems with their identity. Some even talk to Jill and Micah about their feelings.

For Mycah, Sarah, and Leah, support is at home in their mom and dad and each other. But they're willing to share.

Chapter 6

It's a Different World

It's no secret that America is changing. The two fastest-growing groups in the U.S. are Asians and Hispanics. By the year 2000, blacks, Hispanics, Native Americans, and Asians will account for more than 50 percent of the U.S. population. Some areas such as Los Angeles, New York, Chicago, Dallas, and San Antonio have already reached that point.

With society becoming more multiethnic, interracial dating and marriage are becoming more common across all kinds of groups. The number of births of multiracial babies has multiplied 26 times as fast as that of any other group.

We will all experience difficulties as we adjust to this ever-evolving society. There will probably be more growing pains. Change is one thing many people dread. But dread it or not, it is and always will be an inevitable fact of life.

Learning to interact effectively with these other groups will bring about good changes.

Biracial families can play a very important role in this changing world. Today's world is full of hatred, ignorance, and racism. As the racial makeup of society shifts, all are likely to increase. Families like yours can become models of a truly peaceful and creative coexistence. Biracial families are considered by some to be models of racial harmony. That alone should make you prideful.

One day the world may be rid of hatred. Fear may disappear. People may be thought of merely as people, with no concern about the color of their skin or their religion. Having a box to check or classifying people may be a thing of the past.

Many are working for that day; some are fighting against it. Today, you know who you are. You have the best of two worlds. Make the most of them.

Glossary—*Explaining New Words*

biethnic Belonging to two ethnic groups.

biracial Having parents of two races.

classify To arrange in categories.

culture Beliefs, social forms, and traits of a racial, ethnic, national, or social group.

discrimination Prejudices actions or treatment of another person.

ethnic Relating to groups of people classed according to common origins or background.

identity The distinguishing personality of an individual.

interracial Designed for or bringing together several races.

multiracial Having several races in one's family background.

minority Non-white population.

prejudice Poor opinion of a person or group of people formed without grounds or previous knowledge.

racism Prejudice or discrimination against a particular race.

self-esteem Confidence in and satisfaction with one's value to the world.

tradition Cultural continuity in social attitudes and institutions.

Help List

Association for Multi-
cultural Counseling
and Development
5999 Stevenson Avenue
Alexandria, VA 22304

Association of
MultiEthnic
Americans
P.O. Box 191726
San Francisco, CA
94119-1726

Biracial Family Network
P.O. Box 3214
Chicago, IL 60654
(312) 921-1335

Council on Interracial
Books for Children
1841 Broadway
New York, NY 10023

Interracial Family
Alliance
P.O. Box 20290
Atlanta, GA 30325
(404) 696-8113

Interracial Family Circle
P.O. Box 53290
Washington, D.C. 20009

Interracial Intercultural
Pride (I-Pride)
P.O. Box 191752
San Francisco, CA
94119-1752

Multicultural Family
Support Group
466-4 West Reckord
Avenue
Fort Ritchie, MD 21719

Project Race
1425 Market Boulevard
Roswell, GA 30076
(404) 640-7100

For Further Reading

Adoff, Arnold. *Black Is Brown Is Tan*. New York: Harper & Row, 1973.

Almonte, Paul, and Desmond, Theresa. *The Facts About Interracial Marriage*. New York: Crestwood House, 1992.

Bode, Janet. *Different Worlds: Interracial and Cross-Cultural Dating*. New York: Franklin Watts, 1989.

Edwards, Gabrielle I. *Coping with Discrimination*, rev. ed. New York: Rosen Publishing Group, 1992.

Gay, Kathlyn. *The Rainbow Effect: Interracial Families*. New York: Franklin Watts, 1987.

Jones, Lisa. *Bullet-Proof Diva: Tales of Race, Sex, and Hair*. New York: Doubleday, 1994.

Miles, Betty. *All It Takes Is Practice*. New York: Alfred A. Knopf, 1976.

Miller, Maryann. *Coping with a Bigoted Parent*. New York: Rosen Publishing Group, 1992.

Nash, Renea D. *Coping with Interracial Dating*. New York: Rosen Publishing Group, 1993.

Welber, Robert. *The Train*. New York: Pantheon, 1972.

Williams, Garth. *The Rabbit's Wedding*. New York: Harper & Row, 1958.

Index

About the Author
Renea Denise Nash received a bachelor's degree in
journalism from Central Michigan University in 1986.
She earned a master's degree in mass communication
from the Walter Cronkite School of Journalism and
Telecommunication at Arizona State University, where she
was also received the school's outstanding graduate award.
    Ms. Nash has worked for corporate newspapers and
award-winning magazines. She now works as a public
information officer for the city of Phoenix and continues to
write free-lance. Her first book, *Coping with Interracial
Dating*, was published in 1993.

Photo Credits
cover, p. 29 by Lauren Piperno; p. 2 by Kim Sonsky; pp. 6,
10, 47 © AP/Wide World Photo; pp. 9, 21, 39 by Michael
Brandt; pp, 13, 16, 24, 44 by Marcus Shaffer, pp. 34, 50 by
Yung-Hee Chia.